ORGANIC MARKETING

THIS BOOK IS ABOUT HOW TO GROW ORGANICALLY ON FACEBOOK, INSTAGRAM AND YOUTUBE

AF408563

RISHABH PAL

Copyright © Rishabh Pal
All Rights Reserved.

This book has been published with all efforts taken to make the material error-free after the consent of the author. However, the author and the publisher do not assume and hereby disclaim any liability to any party for any loss, damage, or disruption caused by errors or omissions, whether such errors or omissions result from negligence, accident, or any other cause.

While every effort has been made to avoid any mistake or omission, this publication is being sold on the condition and understanding that neither the author nor the publishers or printers would be liable in any manner to any person by reason of any mistake or omission in this publication or for any action taken or omitted to be taken or advice rendered or accepted on the basis of this work. For any defect in printing or binding the publishers will be liable only to replace the defective copy by another copy of this work then available.

Contents

Prologue   *v*

1. Facebook Organic Reach   1

2. Instagram Organic   5

3. Youtube Marketing   6

How I Learnt It   9

How You Can Implement   11

Marketing As A Prince   13

Prologue

In this book we are going to talk about the organic marketing, usually marketers don't want to tell you these things because they want you to give them money to promote your products. These are some of the secrets which nobody tells. This is because organic reach is something free of cost and on the contrary easy to capture your target audience.

This book will include some of the best platforms where you can promote yourself organically.

CHAPTER ONE

FACEBOOK ORGANIC REACH

Facebook is one of the best way to promote yourself. Many people say that facebook is old now, but always I say one thing "did you get all of the users as your followers on facebook page or on your profile" even still if you capture only 1 percent of the total facebook users you will be huge. So, don't underestimate the power of facebook.

Still people are using facebook on regular basis and you will get a good response from them as well.

Here, I am assuming that you know how to create facebook page. Even if you don't know you can go to page option and just go for create a page option.

Starting from the naming of your page, make sure to have the same name as you want your business to be. And make sure to use that name for your business which is somehow related to what your business is.

Here, we are taking an example of our website, Coupleclothes. Instead of clothes you can use a lot of keywords also which relates to your original business. If you are little bit confused about how to make a related word you can also go through keyword planner by google. You will get a good amount knowledge about it also. Like how much people are actually searching for the same name, the average monthly users, etc.

For example, you have take out the related words for clothes.

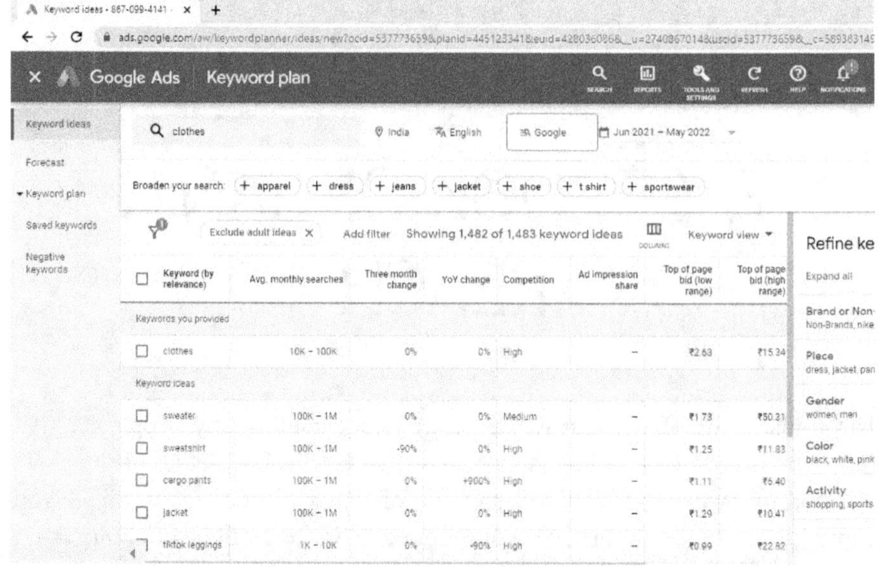

Enter Caption

Now, you will get the all related words with clothes, just see what you need and go with it.

This basically helps your audience to search you and ultimately get you easily.

So, let us start with our next move, how to generate more people towards your facebook page. Have you ever see a live stream on facebook, youtube or anywhere. Do you know why these people are not uploading videos directly, instead of this they are doing live streaming. even they know if there connection would be weak then their audience would leave and join another live stream. Still, instead of directly recording and uploading video they are doing live stream. This is because they know live streams generate more engagement that videos directly uploaded.

Engagement is the player on every platform, the more engagement you get the more you will be popular. Think about it again. Do a live stream, join groups related to what you do. And share your live stream in these groups. Make sure to share your live stream with someone else facebook ID or convince your friends to share in behalf of you.

You must share your videos with others FB ID this is because facebook limit your reach if they know you are sharing in your behalf. This may lead to a problem for you. limited originality of content could also be applied on your page. So, make sure to share with others FB ID.

Now, you have groups. So, you have audience. And if you have audience you can become popular easily on facebook. Just you know the correct strategy of sharing. And its all done.

Always remember in your mind bulk sharing can lead to decrease in your reach. So, make sure to share just little at a time. Bulk sharing can lead to your page downfall. Just make sure to have little sharing at a time. You can continue sharing after some time like 1 or 2 hours.

Following this way you will get good response and reach. You can do the same sharing work with photo, video etc. just you need is audience and the better way to reach them. now you have it. And you can change it now.

Along with this there are several metrics through which you can also earn a good response or reach. Like Hastags.

#Hastags and how they work. Basically, there are different type of hastags people use to follow the and a good amount of posts related to that tag has been shown to their followers. But, there are several things you must know before doing it all. You must not use more than 3 hastags at once, and use all the tags related to each other. In this way you are making a good image in algorithm about your post and will definitely get more reach than before.

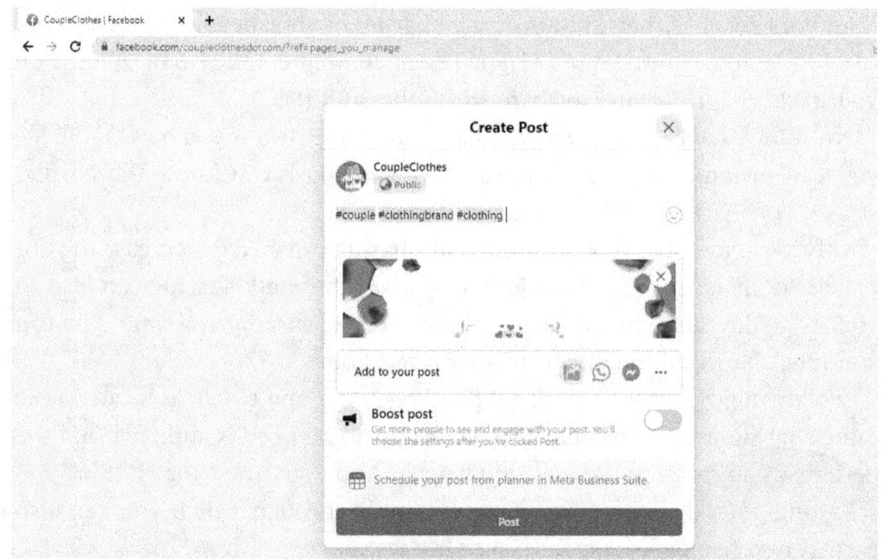

Enter Caption

As you can see here we have used only 3 hastags all related to my brand and now algorithm will understand the post and will show to related users.

If you are not able to find the best hastags to use then all you need to understand the keyword facebook suggests you to use. Find the most probable one and use them.

While using hastags make sure to use those hastags which are more popular and your post at least reach a good amount of people.

CHAPTER TWO

INSTAGRAM ORGANIC

Talking about the Instagram reach, how you can multiply your reach on instagram with no money used. Starting from simple steps, here again I am thinking about you know how to make an account and some basic knowledge about how to use Instagram.

Taking about algorithm, how much I have understood you much have a good quality phone first. This is because good quality interact more with people, even instagram promotes almost every post which is of good quality. This is happening because of one single reason i.e. the engagement, the more good quality content you will produce the more likely you to be good enough to get more views.

Second basic thing is hastags. Again you can use the same strategy for hastags as we have discussed in facebook marketing.

Hastags are more important on instagram as compared to facebook, this is because it helps in generating more and more information for the algorithm of instagram to know more about you and your post, this will ultimately leads to better performance for instagram and for your account as well.

In this way you can easily earn a good audience to your profile.

Another better way is to create reels on the trending songs, you can add anything. Just do a little thing, after adding your video to song make sure to decrease the volume of the song and increase your video volume. In this way the chances for your video to get a good response will be high as compared to any normal video.

Stories are not that efficient until you add something new to it, just do a little task make your story and add the recent trending sticker to it. Like you have seen a lot of time, happy Christmas, new year etc. in this way you story will reach high and the chances of viral makes high.

CHAPTER THREE

YOUTUBE MARKETING

The most easy task you will find is Youtube, getting views on youtube is that easy as you eat food. I had explained it in very brief in my book – Marketing as a Prince, you can easily find it on amazon for 99/-. So, let's talk about youtube marketing now.

Again I am assuming you have basic knowledge of how to create and upload video on youtube. I am just setting a way for you to generate more and more views on youtube.

Go on Ahrefs, a great website where you will find the keywords which are required for you to get a good response. In this way you will get a good response with just using these related keywords only.

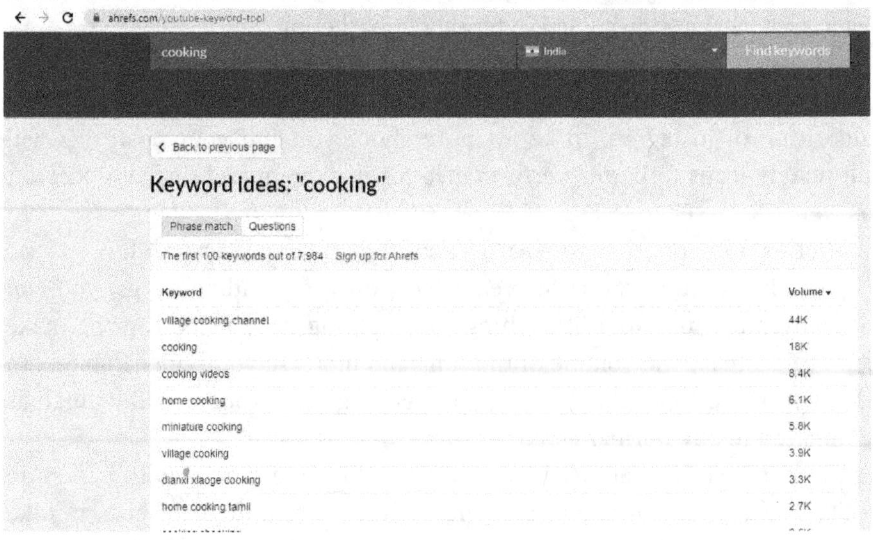

Enter Caption

This is a great way to get more and more views and for a longer period of time. Just use these keywords in your videos and you will get that views that you even haven't think of.

So, there are a lot more things I have shared in my another book name-Marketing as a Prince, you can easily find it on amazon for 99/-. You will get a vast knowledge about these things in a lot more easy way. See you all there. And I can guarantee you that you will find that book a great peace of marketing.

How I Learnt It

This starts with my first website, i don't know how to promote it. then, i look towards digital marketing and some how i found ways to promote myself organically, in this way it all was started. till now i have more than 100 clients for whom i have promoted their products, these are small brands who are somewhere finding a way to promote.

The major part of my work is organic and i suggest each and every one to go organic.

How You Can Implement

The first thing i want to tell you is that, make sure to implement all these things i have told you in this book. and if you continue to do these things i can make sure you will get a good response. better than you are expecting. i have made many millions views on facebook, youtube and on instagram organically, have sold over 70 pages including instagram pages with facebook pages. with over lakhs of followers on it. so, if i can make it you can also make it.

Marketing As A Prince

This is my another book in which i have explained each and everything like you are teaching yourself. i must suggest you to read it once also, it is awesome.

www.ingramcontent.com/pod-product-compliance
Lightning Source LLC
Chambersburg PA
CBHW071230140726
47996CB00004B/1560